The Book of Dorking Chickens
The Mating, Rearing and Management of Different Varieties of Dorkings

by H.H. Stoddard

with an introduction by Jackson Chambers

Self Reliance Books

Get more historic titles on animal and stock breeding, gardening and old fashioned skills by visiting us at:

http://selfreliancebooks.blogspot.com/

Introduction

I am pleased to present yet another title in the "Chicken Breeds" series.

This volume is entitled "The Book of the Dorking" in 1886.

The work is in the Public Domain and is re-printed here in accordance with Federal Laws.

Though this work is a century old it contains much information on poultry that is still pertinent today.

As with all reprinted books of this age that are intended to perfectly reproduce the original edition, considerable pains and effort had to be undertaken to correct fading and sometimes outright damage to existing proofs of this title. At times, this task is quite monumental, requiring an almost total "rebuilding" of some pages from digital proofs of multiple copies. Despite this, imperfections still sometimes exist in the final proof and may detract from the visual appearance of the text.

I hope you enjoy reading this book as much as I enjoyed making it available to readers again.

Jackson Chambers

F. Lydon 1898
The Feathered World

DUCKWING.

PILE.

BLACK-BREASTED RED.

BIRCHEN.

BROWN-BREASTED RED.

GAME BANTAMS.
(Specially drawn to illustrate Mr. Proud's articles on Bantams.)

BLACK ROSECOMB.

JAPANESE.

SILVER AND GOLDEN SEBRIGHTS

BANTAMS.

BRAHMAS.

WHITE ROSECOMB.

BOOTED.

THE BOOK OF THE DORKING.

HISTORICAL.

IN a picturesque valley twenty-nine miles south of London by rail lies the market town of Dorking. It has a population of about five thousand. The town is situated on a small brook, a tributary of the Mole, in a sheltered vale near the base of Box Hill. It is well built and clean. Among its noted buildings are the Parish church of St. Martin's, a handsome edifice, and St. Paul's district church, a building of some pretensions. Several elegant mansions have been erected in the vicinity of the town, notably that of Deepdeen, containing a gallery of sculpture collected by the late Thomas Hope, the author of Anastasius ; near by is also the Rookery where Malthus, celebrated for his essay on population, was born. Lime of exceptionally good quality is burnt to a large extent in the neighborhood, and forms an important article of trade ; it is derived from the Lower Chalk formation. The old Roman road from the Sussex coast to the Thames passed close to the town. Dorking is celebrated throughout England for its romantic scenery, and has long been famous for a finely flavored breed of **fowls,** distinguished by their having five claws upon each foot. These fowls are in great demand in the London markets, and are regarded as the best table fowls produced in the country. They are known by the name of Dorkings, derived from the town which has so long bred them in a high degree of perfection.

The English people are very conservative. The family tree is regarded as the most important of all trees. They really believe that it grew in the Garden of Eden. A long lineage is something to boast of. It is told of a certain noble family that in the portrait gallery there is a picture representing one of their ancestors entering the ark and bearing in his hand a roll containing the family pedigree for centuries previous to the flood. The truth of this story we do not vouch for, but it fittingly represents the feeling of the people. They are fully in harmony with the sentiment, "Old wood to burn! Old wine to drink! Old friends to trust! Old authors to read!" Like Goldsmith, each one says: "I love everything that's old. Old friends, old times, old manners, old books, old wine," and we may add, old varieties of fowls. Unlike the American people, who resemble the ancient Athenians in their rage for something new, age gives, as it ought to, an added value to everything in the eyes of the English. Age does add worth, for it insures stability, and when excellence can boast of age, it becomes even more excellent. It means in poultry that the characteristics have become so fixed as to be uniformly transmitted that we can expect the chick to be like its parents, for its parents are like a long line of ancestors, every one of which possessed the same characteristics. Nothing so tries the patience of the poultry breeder as to find that a fine looking pen of fowls produces a lot of chicks uneven in quality and uncertain in characteristics, resembling neither themselves nor their progenitors. And this is the result to be expected from new breeds.

The Dorking is the most popular fowl in England. It boasts of a long lineage. It traces its origin to a time when England was not a nation, when the inhabitants of that now most highly civilized country were painted savages. It antedates royalty. Before William the Conqueror, the Dorking was; before the battle of Hastings, the Dorking had conquered popularity. It takes us back to the ancient city of Rome, "which sat upon her seven hills and ruled the world;" it brings us to the fountain of jurisprudence, to the foundations of order and society. In comparison, other breeds are puny upstarts without a pedigree, the *noveau riche*, the plebeian nobility, made and unmade by a royal word. It is the most patrician of the patricians, the noblest of the nobles, the most regal of the royal families.

It is supposed that the Dorkings were introduced into Britain by the Romans. Along with the conquering cohorts of Cæsar, marched the equally victorious Dorking. The walls that were built, the fortifications that were erected and the roads that were made still bear witness to the Roman invasion; and no less so does this celebrated breed of fowls. In very early Latin writings we find a description of fowls, both white and colored, that accurately represents this breed. Columella has thus clearly described the modern Colored Dorking: "Let them be of reddish or dark plumage, with black wings.

*   *   *   *   *   Let the breeding hens be of robust body, square built, full breasted, large heads, with upright and bright red combs.   *   *   *   *   * Those are believed to be the best bred with five toes."

There has always been a dispute as to which was the more ancient variety of Dorkings, the White or the Colored. As both varieties are known to have existed, if we may rely upon the ancient writers who have given a description of a fowl which fits the Dorking, at so early a date as to leave their origin in the mythical period which precedes the dawn of history, no satisfactory settlement of this dispute is likely to be arrived at. The difficulty remains an insoluble one. The advocates of the claims of the White to priority urge that the Colored Dorking was produced by a cross of the White variety upon the ancient Sussex fowl, and instance the fact that some strains of Colored Dorkings were very uncertain in the production of the fifth toe ; the advocates of the Colored Dorking, on the other hand, claim that, as the Colored surpasses the White variety in size, the White is, therefore, but a degenerate descendant of the older variety. Mr. Martin Doyle, the author of " The Illustrated Book of Domestic Poultry," makes the following ingenious suggestion : " If we may venture to offer a conjecture on this abstract point of physiology, we should say that as in vegetable propagation, white flowers are often found to break or degenerate into colors, although colored flowers do not become pure white,— so, by analogy, the white bird would degenerate into a colored one though the converse would be unnatural." This explanation we cannot, however, accept. Analogies are always dangerous things to rely upon, especially when, as in this case, they are drawn from different kingdoms of the created world. We know that white birds are constantly appearing as " sports " among colored ones, but never knew of the converse. White crows, white blackbirds, white sparrows, white Spanish, white Langshans, white Javas, white Plymouth Rocks, white Wyandottes, have frequently appeared, but who can cite a well authenticated case where a colored domesticated bird appeared among white ones, when it could not be shown to have come from a cross or was the result of reversion? White feathers are easy to get and hard to get rid of. If the Colored Dorking sprang from the White variety, as some eminent authorities believe, it resulted from a cross and not otherwise; but the White Dorking might have appeared as a "sport." We are willing to allow this question to remain unsettled, claiming no superiority of antiquity for either White or Colored Dorkings.

VARIETIES.

In this country three varieties of Dorkings are recognized by the *Standard*, the White, the Silver Gray, and the Colored. In size the White is the smallest of the three, the Colored the largest, and the Silver Gray intermediate between the two. The White is bred with a rose comb only, the other two varieties with either rose or single combs, although the greater number of Colored and Silver Gray Dorkings, both in this country and in England, their native home, are bred with single combs.

All three varieties, with the above exceptions and with the added one of color and marking, possess the same characteristics. They all have white or flesh colored legs, five toes upon each foot, white skins, long bodies, full breasts, heavy thighs, small bones and are wonderfully compact and meaty in their make-up. As an old writer describes them, " These fowles have very short legges, and are small boned throughout, and the offal is very light, consequently the proportion of flesh is very large."

Mr. Baily, an eminent London poultry judge, says that " There is no breed to be compared with the Dorking, which unites in itself, more than any other, all the properties requisite for supplying the table ; that the hens are good sitters and good mothers, and that there is a natural tendency in the breed to fatten, so that the young ones are made to attain to eight or nine pounds' weight, and at table they surpass all others in symmetry of shape, and whiteness, and delicacy of flesh."

The Rev. E. S. Dixon writes : " For those who wish to stock their poultry-yard with fowls of the most desirable shape and size, clothed in rich and variegated plumage, and not expecting perfection, the speckled (i. e., Colored) Dorkings are the breed to be at once selected. The hens, in addition to their gay colors, have a large vertically flat comb, which, when they are in high health, adds very much to their brilliant appearance, particularly if seen in bright sunshine. The cocks are magnificent ; the most gorgeous hues are frequently lavished upon them, which their great size and peculiarly square-built form display to the greatest advantage. The breeder, and the farmer's wife, behold with delight their broad breast, the small proportion of offal, and the large quantity of

WHITE DORKING FOWLS.

(11)

profitable flesh. The cockerels may be brought to considerable weights, and the flavour and appearance of the meat are inferior to none. The eggs are produced in reasonable abundance, and though not equal in size to those of Spanish hens, may fairly be called large. They are not everlasting layers, but at due and convenient intervals manifest the desire of sitting. In this respect they are steady, and good mothers when the little ones appear."

Another writer says of them, that "of all domestic fowls with which he was acquainted, the Dorkings must carry off the palm for their good size and lofty carriage, for the beauty and variety of their plumage, and, lastly, for their exceptional table qualities."

Mr. L. Wright, an eminent poultry author, thus describes the Dorking: "The body should be deep and full, the breast being protuberant and plump, especially in the cock, whose breast, as viewed sideways, ought to form a right angle with the lower part of his body. Both back and breast must be broad, the latter showing no approach to hollowness, and the entire general make full and plump, but neat and compact. Hence a good bird should weigh more than it appears to do."

These descriptions ought to bring before the reader's imagination a fowl in which solidity is a pre-eminent quality, whose peculiar figure fits it for the table. No better shape could be devised for this purpose, as it provides for little waste in comparison with the amount of flesh.

May we not, in view of the mania of our people for new varieties, echo the sentiment of the editor of the

WHITE DORKING CHICKS.

Agricultural Gazette, who said of Mr. Baily, that " he should be encouraged in his endeavor to bring us back to Dorkings and common sense ?"

THE WHITE DORKING.

The White Dorking, by some regarded as the oldest of all varieties of Dorkings, has the general characteristics of all the varieties. In plumage it is pure white, although there is more or less tendency in cocks to become somewhat yellow upon the back, hackle and saddle. This is a characteristic of all white fowls. It is bred only with a rose comb, which should be square in front, fit firmly and evenly upon the head, be comparatively flat upon the top and evenly covered with small points, and terminate in a large spike or projection behind, which should curve slightly upwards. The carriage should be elegant and stately. An old writer upon the subject of Dorkings, as quoted by Mr. George T. Goodwin, an enthusiastic and eminent breeder of Dorkings, says : " This variety seldom attains the large size of the darker shades, but this does not prove any inferiority. For general use we do not advise this variety, unless the location should be on a dry and sandy soil, as success in breeding would require constant attention to prevent any discoloration of feather. This disadvantage is no greater than in other pure white varieties, and the fowls have also the great advantage of the small bones and tender flesh so peculiar to this breed, in all its varieties."

Upon a lawn a white fowl shows off to great advantage, and the goodly size, even though less than that of the other varieties, the plump, compact figure, the bright

SILVER GRAY DORKINGS.

(15)

red comb and wattles contrasting with the pure white plumage, make the White Dorking a fine appearing fowl where it can have a good grass run.

THE SILVER GRAY DORKING.

The Silver Gray Dorking originated without doubt from the Colored variety. In a brood of Colored Dorking chicks there frequently appears one or more that are much lighter in color than the others. The selection of these lighter chicks as breeding stock in time produced this variety.

Although descended from the Colored variety they are hardly as large as that variety, but larger than the White.

The Silver Gray cock has the head, neck, and back clad in a plumage of silvery whiteness. The wing-bows are also silvery white. The breast is a rich, glossy black; the wing-coverts are a metallic black with a greenish lustre, and form a wide bar across the wing; the tail is large and full, and of a rich black color, the sickle-feathers having a green lustre; the tail-coverts are of a glossy black, the lesser coverts having an edging of white. The under parts of the body and the thighs are also black.

The Silver Gray hen has a silvery white neck, silvery or slaty gray back, salmon-red breast shading off to gray towards the sides, silvery or slaty gray body, dark gray tail, and ashy gray thighs.

Both cock and hen are clad in a handsome plumage, and the appearance of the cock is especially striking.

COLORED DORKINGS.

(37)

THE COLORED DORKING.

The Colored Dorking cock closely resembles the Silver Gray in plumage, and the one is easily mistaken for the other by the casual observer. The hackle of the Colored cock displays a broad black stripe down the center of each feather; the breast is sometimes splashed with white, although a solid black breast is preferred; the wing-bows are white or sometimes mixed with black; the back is black and white; but in all other respects the plumage of the Colored Dorking cock is like that of the Silver Gray.

The Colored hen has a black or nearly black head, the feathers of the neck black edged with gray, the back dark gray marked with black, the breast dark salmon marked with black, body dark brown, tail dark brown or gray on the outside, black on the inside, and the thighs dark gray or brown. She is darker throughout in her plumage than her Silver Gray sister.

The *Standard* fixes no weights for the White and Silver Gray varieties, but for the Colored it gives the following :

Cock, 9½ lbs.	Hen, 7½ lbs.
Cockerel, 8 lbs.	Pullet, 6 lbs.

These weights are rather high, although occasional specimens are found to exceed them. A cock which weighs 8 lbs. and a hen which weighs 6 lbs. may be regarded as good birds. Cocks have been known to reach 12 lbs. in weight and hens 9 lbs., but such instances are rare, and the great weight was due to excessive fatness.

THE DORKING AS AN EGG PRODUCER.

The Dorking lays a good-sized, white egg with a slight creamy tint, not pronounced enough to be called a colored egg. The eggs are of a good flavor and excellent for culinary purposes. But they are not produced in so great abundance as one could wish. The fowl's chief claim is for its admirable table qualities. It has been bred for this purpose for centuries, and it would be nothing surprising if prolificacy should have been overlooked. And yet among Dorkings some hens will be found that are prolific layers. There is a record of a Dorking hen which laid one hundred and eighteen eggs in one hundred and twenty-one days, a record not easily broken even by the Leghorns or Hamburgs.

Mr. Martin Doyle, in his "Illustrated Book of Domestic Poultry," furnishes a series of interesting tables showing the comparative merit of four breeds of fowls as producers of eggs. From this series we make the following table.

Hatched April 10th, 1851.	When began to lay, 1851.	Number of eggs laid to April 10th, 1852.	Number of eggs laid from April 10th, 1852, to April 10th, 1853.	Total number of eggs laid during two years from date of hatching.	Total weight of eggs.
					oz.
4 Shanghais,	Oct. 19,	709	1059	1768	3569
4 Spanish,	Dec. 7,	452	928	1380	3456
4 Dorkings,	Dec. 1,	471	969	1440	3004
4 Polish,	Nov. 26,	512	885	1397	2961

An examination of this table shows that from the date of hatching until the fowls were two years old four Dorking hens laid 1,440 eggs or an average of 360 eggs each, which would be 180 eggs per year, but if we reckon the laying from the time when they began to lay, viz., December 1st, we shall have as the actual laying time but one year, four months and ten days, or at the rate of over 249 eggs each per year, a rate which even the best strains of Leghorns seldom equal.

In our own experience we have found Colored Dorking hens that were exceptionally good layers, but as a rule Dorkings are not the best of layers. By selecting from these extra layers eggs for hatching and continuing to follow this practice for a number of years, a strain of Dorking hens possessing extraordinary prolificacy might be established. There is good material to build on, and we can see no reason why success might not crown the wisely directed efforts of any breeder who has persistency as one of his endowments.

AS A TABLE FOWL

the Dorking acknowledges no superior. The flesh is disposed just where it is most wanted; it is juicy, tender, and of delicious flavor. As Mr. Goodwin says: "No man knows better than an English Squire that when he has a bird of this breed properly cooked and served on his board, he has the best that the kingdom affords." Mr. L. Wright, than whom there is no better authority, says: "The great merit of Dorkings has already been hinted at, and consists in their unrivalled excellence as table fowls. In this respect we never expect to see them

COLORED DORKINGS BRED BY V. A. BLAKESLEE, WINSTED, CONN.

(21)

surpassed. The meat is not only abundant and of good quality, surpassing any other English breed except Game, but is produced in the greatest quantity in the choicest parts—breast, merry-thought and wings. Add to this, that no breed is so easily got into good condition for the table, and enough has been said to justify the popularity of this beautiful English fowl."

We might multiply quotations to the same effect for many pages, but enough already has been said to point out the simple fact that for the table the Dorking stands without a rival.

CAPONS.

Caponizing a fowl is the same thing as castrating a calf. We shall not attempt a description of the process, as no one would undertake it without procuring a suitable set of instruments, and with each set of instruments complete printed instructions are sent. The operation is not a difficult one to perform, and a little practice would enable one to become quite skillful in it. It is surprising that more capons are not made, for there can be no more profitable way of disposing of the extra cockerels that are annually reared and not wanted for breeding purposes. No variety of fowl is better suited for this purpose than the Dorking, especially the Colored Dorking. Delicious capons of great size could be reared that in the city markets would command a very high price. We think the time is not far distant when this branch of the poultry industry will be better understood, and when capons will be more abundant than they now are. As our population more and more centers in the cities, the demand for "a good fat capon" will be increased; and as the merits of the Colored Dorking for this purpose become better known the demand for them will become still greater.

CROSSING.

We do not believe in keeping cross-bred fowls, and yet it cannot be denied that great advantages arise to the market poulterer from crossing. By the purchase of a single cock the value of his year's produce may be greatly increased. For market purposes a Dorking cock can be confidently recommended. The farmer may keep for instance a flock of Leghorn hens to supply him with an abundance of eggs. With these he can allow a Dorking cock to run, and while the supply of eggs is not diminished the value of his chicks, for market, both on account of the greater size and the improved quality, is very appreciably increased. The Dorking crossed with any of the large breeds, the Brahmas and Cochins, produces an admirable table-fowl, the Dorking blood improving greatly the quality of the flesh, and rendering the fowl more easily fattened for the table. The rearing of market poultry has not received that attention in this country which its importance demands, and which it is destined to receive in the near future. When that time comes, as come it must, we shall find many cross-bred fowls which owe their excellence as table-fowls to the blood of the Dorking.

THE DORKING AS AN INCUBATOR AND BROODER.

There is no better sitter than a quiet Dorking hen. Objection has been made to the fifth toe as more liable to break the eggs or tread upon the chickens, but experience proves this objection utterly unfounded. In a season when other hens brought off broods of five and six chickens, we have hatched under a Colored Dorking hen every egg. As mothers they are exemplary. They run with their chickens longer than many varieties, and take excellent care of them. As incubators and brooders we can recommend them as "equalled by few and surpassed by none."

TAMENESS.

We have found the Dorking a fowl that can be easily rendered tame. This is a quality frequently overlooked in making the choice of a breed, but one which counts for much in the satisfaction to be derived from keeping fowls. Some varieties are naturally shy, and although subjected to the kindest treatment, the sudden appearance of the owner will set them wildly flying in every direction. But Dorkings are unlike this. They welcome the presence of their attendant and crowd around him whenever he appears. They are frequently very amusing in their ways. We had a Colored Dorking hen that would come running up to us, and would pick at the buttons on our shoes until we took her up and petted her, and then she would seem contented, as if she had gained the attention that she felt she deserved. One soon becomes very much attached to a flock of tame fowls, and would not willingly part with them. And there is something more than sentiment in this quality. It is a very great convenience. It is often necessary to examine a fowl closely, and it is very try-

COLORED DORKINGS.

(25)

ing to the patience and temper to be obliged to spend a quarter of an hour in the pursuit of a bird, and then perhaps not succeed in catching it. When one has tried this he quickly wishes that he owned a flock with a different disposition, and he is quite likely to feel the necessity of making a change in the breed kept. We have never known any one, for this reason, to wish to change his Dorkings for any other variety.

MATING.

In mating White Dorkings, it is necessary to select birds having a pure white plumage, with no colored feathers, a good comb, not too large, and setting squarely upon the head, and birds of the largest size obtainable. The smaller size of this variety has been one of the greatest obstacles to its achieving the popularity that it really deserves. We believe that the size might be improved by mating with a White cock some of the lightest colored hens of the Silver Gray variety. From such a mating some pure white chicks would be obtained, and a cockerel from these could be bred back to White hens. A few colored feathers might appear in the second generation, but by selecting only pure white specimens of this generation to breed from, and mating them again with White birds, in the third generation colored feathers would probably not appear, and the breeder would be amply repaid in the increased size of the fowls.

In Silver Grays it is essential not only that the cock and hens should be of the standard colors and markings, but should be bred from Silver Grays themselves. In a flock of Colored Dorkings, Silver Gray chicks occasionally appear, but they cannot be relied upon for the breeding of Silver Grays. Many of the chicks from such a pen, from the operation of the law of reversion, will throw back to their grandparents, and will resemble the Colored Dorking in color and marking. The cock should have a pure silvery white hackle, free from any black stripe, saddle, wing-bows and back of the same character, and a solid black breast. The hens should be of large size, and of standard color. In all matings of Dorkings the size of the hens is an important matter. Upon the hen, more than upon the cock, depends the size of the chicks.

In mating Colored Dorkings the black stripe in the hackle and saddle-feathers is to be insisted upon, and a plentiful admixture of black upon the back and wing-bows is essential. If the hackle has the broad black stripe, the back and the wing-bows will be of the desired character. We prefer that the cock should have a solid black breast, other things being equal, but a good bird otherwise is not to be rejected because the breast is slightly mottled. The hens should be well broken in feather, the black markings being clearly discernible, and they should be of good size, and of standard color.

In mating both Silver Grays and Colored Dorkings, the cocks and hens should have the same kind of comb, rose combs being mated to rose combs, and single combs with single combs.

In all varieties of Dorkings the peculiar shape of the body, a well defined parallelogram, the characteristic fifth toe, and the white or flesh-colored leg, are matters not to be overlooked.

Such matings will produce chicks that will show a good percentage of birds, when matured, that are fit for the exhibition room or the breeding pen.

NUMBER OF HENS TO COCK.

The number of hens to cock will vary somewhat according to the activity of the cock. An active cockerel, about one year old, will answer for about ten hens. An old cock ought not to be allowed more than five or six. We prefer a cockerel mated to hens two or three years old, allowing him eight or ten. If pullets are used, we should prefer to mate them with a good two year old cock. Avoid, so far as possible, mating young birds together, *i. e.* pullets with a cockerel. The very best mating is of a cockerel about one year old with large two or three year old hens. The chicks from an old hen's eggs are larger and stronger when first hatched, and this advantage they maintain at all stages of growth. Chicks from the eggs of pullets never overtake those from the eggs of hens, and the losses in rearing are much larger. This is a matter the importance of which is to a great extent overlooked, but the breeder cannot afford to neglect it. Each year the most promising pullets should be saved and kept among the laying stock, and the next year from them the breeding stock should be selected.

INBREEDING.

Avoid inbreeding. No fowls deteriorate more rapidly when inbred than the Dorkings. Fresh blood is indispensable, if size and hardiness is to be kept up. The breeder of Dorkings should either keep enough pens of breeding stock to insure the introduction of fresh blood annually, or should each year purchase a good male bird from the yards of some responsible breeder. It will pay him to do so. He will get more and better chicks by so doing. If we were to condense the subject of the successful breeding of Dorkings into three principles, we should name them as follows :

First. *Fresh blood!*
Second. FRESH BLOOD !!
Third. FRESH BLOOD !!! ·

Nothing is of greater importance than this, and too much stress cannot be laid upon it.

THE CHICK.

The White Dorking chick is, of course, white in color when first hatched. The Silver Gray and Colored Dorking chicks are of brownish gray color, with well defined stripes on their backs, like the chipmunks of New England. They are " sleek, line-backed, five-toed beauties." The wing-feathers appear at a very early age and show the characteristic gray color. All Dorking chicks, from the earliest age, display the characteristic Dorking shape.

As chicks they are somewhat delicate to rear, although hardy as fowls, and should not be hatched either too early or too late in the season. We have met with the best success in May and June hatched chicks, preferring these months to all others for this purpose. Hatched at this time they thrive, and but few die. They grow rapidly and mature quite early, and are fit for the spit

at almost any age. They make the best of broilers, because of their meaty qualities. They can be used for
this purpose at the age of about eight weeks, and from
that time on are ready for market at any period of
their growth.

Dry feeding is the best. Our plan of feeding is as
follows: The chicks are left undisturbed until about
twenty-four hours old. They are then removed with their
mother to a suitable coop, and are fed for four or five
days upon hard boiled eggs, chopped very fine and
mixed with bread crumbs. Fresh water is kept constantly before them. At the expiration of four or five
days we give them steam-cooked oatmeal dry, such as is
purchased for family use, and in the state that it is obtained from the grocer, alternating with fine cracked
corn. As soon as they are old enough to eat it, we
vary this diet with whole wheat. Cracked bone and
oyster shells are kept constantly before them. Ground
beef scraps are fed about every other day. Milk, sweet
or sour, is given them for drink when we have it. We
should like to keep it constantly before them. In case
the chicks appear to droop, we give them an occasional
boiled egg, chopped fine, with a little Indian meal wet
up thick with boiling water and seasoned slightly with
cayenne pepper, but we find this very seldom necessary.

For the first two or three weeks we feed our chicks
five times a day, in the morning, in the middle of the
forenoon, at noon, in the middle of the afternoon, and
at night. After that we feed three times a day until
well grown.

We keep a sharp outlook for lice. Nothing so saps

the vitality of a chick as the presence of lice. They are generally to be found upon the head, burrowing into the skull. If the chick is not very closely examined, their presence will not be detected. When a chick begins to droop, even if an examination does not disclose any lice, it is perfectly safe to grease the head thoroughly with lard. For lice we use lard, sulphur, or Persian Insect Powder, each separately, but never in combination. Sulphur and lard combined we regard as deadly to chicks, an opinion reached by the experience of the loss of two whole broods which we had annointed with the mixture. Dry sulphur thoroughly sprinkled through the down, or Persian Insect Powder so used, will cause the vermin to disappear. Greasing the head alone we have found very effectual.

With this kind of care we have succeeded in rearing whole broods without the loss of a single chick. Other methods of feeding and care may be equally good, but we are satisfied from actual trial that this is good enough. We have tried other methods but none that gave us better satisfaction.

EXHIBITING DORKINGS.

In matching Dorkings for exhibition great care is essential. It is necessary in the White variety that the plumage should be pure white, free from colored feathers, and from all stains. It is justifiable and necessary sometimes to wash the birds before exhibiting them. They should be carefully dried and kept warm, so that no cold will be taken after the washing. Size is very important, and the largest birds of the best shape should be selected.

The combs should be rose, and those of the hens should be as nearly of one size as possible, and of both cock and hens such as are described in the *Standard*. The legs of both cock and hens should be of the same shade of color, and the characteristic fifth toe should be found on all the fowls.

In Silver Grays, the cock should show no black in hackle, back, saddle or wing-bows. His breast and under parts should be solid black. The hens should match in color and size. The combs may be either rose or single, but should be the same upon both cock and hens; they all should have rose combs or single combs.

In Colored Dorkings, the cock should weigh 9½ lbs. or more, the hen 7½ lbs., and in chicks the cockerel should weigh 8 lbs. and the pullet 6 lbs. These are the standard weights, and it is well to have exhibition birds full on weight, especially as this point counts twelve in the score. The cock may have a mottled breast, but a solid black one is preferred and stands a better chance of winning. The hackle should have a broad black stripe down the center; many Colored Dorking cocks fail in this, but as this is one of the distinctions between the Colored and Silver Gray, it is well to insist upon it. The markings and colors should be according to the requirements of the *Standard*. The hens should match in color and size, and both cock and hens should match in combs, all having either single or rose combs.

In judging Dorkings, special attention is given to Symmetry, Size, Comb, Breast and Body, forty-two points out of a possible hundred being allowed for these parts. While other parts are not to be neglected in selecting exhibition birds, it is well to select those that are as nearly perfect as possible in these parts. After these, be careful for Back, Wings and Tail. Condition is also another point to be specially regarded, and the birds should be in perfect health and full plumage.

THE SUPERIORITY OF THE COLORED OVER OTHER VARIETIES OF DORKINGS.

While we admire all varieties of Dorkings, we place first in our estimation the Colored variety. We do so for the following reasons :

1st. They are the largest variety. The Dorking being first of all bred for its flesh, size is the most important of all the qualities. Too much breeding to feather has somewhat reduced the size of the Silver Gray, although it originated from the Colored Dorking. It is still a noble bird, and of good size, but seldom attains the great weight that is reached by the finest specimens of the Colored variety.

2d. They are the hardiest. Too much inbreeding, to fix the color of the Silver Gray, has not only reduced its size, but has diminished its hardiness. This has not been the case with the Colored Dorking. Greater latitude in feathering has been allowed, and breeders have selected the largest and hardiest specimens for their breeding pens.

3d. We think the plumage of the Colored superior to that of the Silver Gray or White. The hackle of cocks especially is very handsome, the broad black stripe adding much to the beauty of the feathering.

4th. We believe the Colored the most prolific variety. The causes which have operated to reduce the hardiness and size of the other varieties, have also been effective in reducing their prolificacy. The best egg record among the Dorkings have, so far as we know, been made by hens of the Colored variety. Experience and theory seem to clasp hands upon this matter. If ever a great laying strain of Dorkings is produced, something within the realm of possibility, we believe it will be from careful selection of Colored hens.

CONCLUSION.

We confess to a love for this good old variety. We are not an "anglo-maniac." We are not ashamed of our birth in this country. We love our free institutions, which place every man upon a level of possibility. We admire American breeds of fowls, especially that distinctive production known as the Plymouth Rock. But we confess, also, to a love for what is excellent and old. As John Webster wrote in 1638: "Is not old wine wholesomest, old pippins toothsomest, old wood burns brightest, old linen wash whitest? Old soldiers, sweetheart, are surest, and old lovers soundest." The Dorking is the oldest variety of fowls. Many varieties have sprung up and died. The path of time is strewed with their wrecks. But the Dorking, because of its intrinsic merits, has survived. It has brought its popularity with it, and those that once have bred it, cling to their first love. They fear Cupid's curse:

> "My merry, merry, merry roundelay
>   Concludes with Cupid's curse:
> They that do change old love for new,
>   Pray gods, they change for worse."

The many excellent qualities of the Dorking have helped to endow other breeds with sufficient excellence to allow them to survive. Much of the good that is occasionally found in the mongrel stock of the farm yard has been derived from the blood of the Dorking. The new has its roots in the old,

> " For out of old fieldes, as men saithe,
>   Cometh al this new corne fro yere to yere
> And out of old bookes, in good faithe,
>   Cometh al this new science that men lere."

And out of the Dorking have sprung qualities that have helped new breeds on to recognition, and enabled them to win success.

To the lovers of fine-bred poultry, to those who believe in a long pedigree, to those who are fond of the delights of a good table, to those who desire fowls for pets, to those who wish for the union of utility and beauty, the oldest, the most aristocratic of all breeds of domestic poultry, the Dorking can be confidently recommended.